Advertising

Your Business

Business Advertising Blueprint: The Complete Guide to Build a Profitable Business and Get Exposure with The Power of Advertising

Robert Hill

Table of Contents

INTRODUCTION 1

CHAPTER 1 7

HOW TO CREATE A SUCCESSFUL ADVERTISING PLAN 7

GET YOUR CREATIVE JUICES FLOWING IF YOU WANT TO CREATE GOOD
ADVERTISEMENT'S.. 11

CHAPTER 2 15

HOW TO WRITE GOOD ADVERTISING CONTENT?.......................... 15

ADVERTISING USING POWER WORDS 19

CHAPTER 3 24

CHARACTERISTICS OF A SUCCESSFUL ADVERTISEMENT 24

RESEARCH IN ADVERTISING 28

CHAPTER 4 32

ADVERTISING FOR FREE... 32

SEARCH ENGINE OPTIMIZATION AND ADVERTISING..................... 35

CHAPTER 5 41

WRITING A GOOD HEADLINE FOR YOUR ADVERTISEMENT........ 41

CHAPTER 6 45

LOW-COST ADVERTISING.. 45

ADVERTISING ON INTERNET... 49

CHAPTER 7 55

HOW TO WRITE BUSINESS-TO-BUSINESS ADVERTISEMENT 55

IMPACT OF COLOURS IN ADVERTISEMENTS.................................. 58

ADVERTISING: SELF PROMOTION 61

CHAPTER 8 67

OTHER ADVERTISING OPTIONS... 67

ADVERGAMING: ADVERTISING THROUGH VIDEO GAMES 67

ADVERTISING FOR FREE 70

ADVERTISING IN YELLOW PAGES 73

ADVERTISING ON INTERNET 76

ADVERTISING ON TELEVISION 80

ADVERTISING: SELF PROMOTION 83

ADVERTISING USING POWER WORDS 87

BILLBOARD ADVERTISING 90

CELEBRITY BRANDING 93

LOW BUDGET ADVERTISING 96

CONCLUSION **101**

Introduction

There are a lot of methods out there to help you learn the most effective ways to advertise your business.

Some work... Most do not.

Unfortunately, most methods promise the world, but just do not deliver on helping and teaching you to get the results that you want. But what if there was a guide that would very quickly get you the results you are wanting. Not just for the short term, but for the long term too.

Not only that but helping you learn the correct mindset and knowledge in advertising methods for your business, so you can see the results you have been wanting.

If you are planning to start advertising your business or have started and failing in the process than you need a guide that can provide you with everything to help you succeed. So, let me introduce you to this fantastic book.

A guide that is jammed packed with tried and tested methods, so you can see results fast.

There are so many products available in teaching you how to advertise your business, making it a challenge to know what the best solution is for you.

These resources can be helpful, and it is a great idea to research each one of them to know what will work best for you and what methods you should use.

But what you are needing is a convenient all-in-one resource that will help you to become more knowledgeable in this subject before you begin.

That is why this new guide all about advertising your business the correct way is a guide that covers all these topics in one.

This is an easy-to-follow guide, and anyone can use it to start learning everything there is to know about this subject. So, whether you are already have tried advertising your business or planning to start, then this product will guide you through the main principals to help you master everything there is to know about this subject. Do not wait and end up missing out.

Most of the professionals in the advertising industry agree to the fact that obtaining a degree is not a must to get started in the industry, but on the contrary all the classifieds ask for a bachelor's degree at least. Another advantage of taking a degree is that if internship is taken during the course, it will provide adequate experience that ad agencies and companies usually ask for.

The internship director of the university can help in this regard. He may have links that could make it possible to get a break in radio, television or even in an ad agency, the choice totally depends on interest.

In case the internship director is of no help, become a part of a network and get to know people around you. This will surely land you somewhere. It will not hurt to search for an internship on your own.

Check out the local newspapers for classifieds; call up local radio and television stations and even ad agencies inquiring about any vacancies. Usually there are lots of ads in the Sunday edition of newspaper, drop in a resume at their office. Best idea is to get in contact with the production manager or the news director of the company. Send them a mail; give a good reference, which can be of big help.

Usually there are lots of chances for internships in the production department. If there is any success in finding an internship, bring it to the notice of the internship director; most probably her reference can be of some advantage.

If these attempts do not work, volunteer to work for free at any local fair, functions and events. Display your creativity to the fullest. This can catch the attention of someone important sometime who can give you that jump-start.

For people who do not opt for regular college, they can always find lots of material related to advertising on the Internet. Other than studying the theory work, try to observe the work of famous personalities in the industry.

Get some ideas, mix it with some creativity and create some original work and approach the local radio station or television channel. Since there are number of shows running there will be some kind of a vacancy.

Get a chance at cross-training too. If initially a job was provided with other shows at the station, try to switch to advertising after winning impression. After getting a break into advertising, it will automatically increase the exposure to the advertising industry and even to other ad agencies.

This will be a good point on the resume, as most of the employers get impressed with television experience. And when working on your first job, there will be a great chance of learning the basics, so do not hesitate to explore the ground.

But since it is easier to get a job here and there is lots of competition for that post, the returns are not that good and there is no job security.

After getting good experience whether it is internship or local radio or television station, resume is the next important step. Fill it up with creativity as that is the main essence of this field. Do not forget to include past experience, even if it is small or not related exactly to the job description, recommendation, if any. The more information added, the stronger the resume and the easier it is to manoeuvre to the top.

Chapter 1

How to Create a Successful Advertising Plan

M any factors have to be considered when making an advertising plan.

Like the type of message to be delivered, the audience to be targeted, how they should be targeted, budget, etc. all of which depends on the nature of the advertisement.

Regarding the type of message to be delivered, try thinking from the point of customer. What will impress him and catch his fancy. Note down points what the customer expects from the company and what advantage will he have when dealing with the company.

Effort should be made to retain viewer or listener's or reader's interest in the advertisement until the end. This procedure is known as message selection.

After creating the outline of the picture, pick lines that will actually attract the customer. The message should not be long enough to bore the customer. Some advertisers are under illusion that more the matter written, the better the message delivered. Usually, they fear that they do not miss out any information. This does nothing but decreases the effectiveness of the ad and customer is left unsatisfied.

For example, the heading of the advertisement should not be just "We Sell Clothes", which is too precise. The liking of the people should be studied, and the headline should be designed such that the customer feels that his needs are met.

It should also take into consideration seasonal changes like If the season at that time is summer and there are lots of beaches around that area, the heading of the ad should be something like "Summer Clothes for Sale" or "Get the heat off - Buy Swimwear".

The body of the advertisement should talk of the necessities to switch to summer clothes like cotton clothing. It should discuss the health point of view too, like cotton cannot be used as swimwear as it will cause contamination, therefore swimwear is made of synthetic material.

Also include lines about swimwear for overweight people. Ads are either traffic builder or relationship builders or reputation builder. Suppose the budget involved is less, target should be relationship builder.

Because once the customers are established, they will start trusting the company and will not switch to other companies.

According to a research it takes ten percent less resources to retain existing customers than attracting new customer. If the focus is on brand recognition, the advertisement should be traffic building.

The next point is whether the advertiser wants quick results or long-lasting results. If quick result is desired, then a time limit should be levied. Like in case of seasonal sales, the customer hurries to get advantage before the offer is over.

So quick results are expected in this case. But the disadvantage with advertisement with time limit is that the customer is bound to forget about the product or the company within a short period and it does not create a deep impact on the minds of the customer.

Competing against rival company's ad also contributes to a successful advertising plan. The power of the message should be compared to that of the competitors.

It does not mean that advertiser should use the same plan as his competitor, it would look like imitation and effectiveness will be decreased. But the advertisement should be planned smartly via a different, effective path, to out-do competitor's advertisement.

The description of the product is also very vital like suppose an advertisement is made for a restaurant, it will get customers immediately, if it is attractive. But if advertisement is for a computer, it will not yield immediate results, as it is not every day that someone buys a computer. This is called analysis of the purchase cycle.

If targeting for a higher impact, newsletter is the best bet. But if the newsletters are sent to the real potential customers, then this approach should be adopted for message delivery. It should only be opted be after thorough analysis, no matter what the budget is. Another important point is to always hire a very professional advertiser or an ad writer because not hiring one will sometimes be more expensive and results in more losses.

Get Your Creative Juices Flowing If You Want to Create Good Advertisements

Those who do not have creativity as an in-built talent, it takes some hard work to learn the art of advertising. There are some really basic tricks involved.

First, try to put things that you have, to use i.e., the five senses along with the brain. Eyes can capture the most beautiful scenes; try remembering those that are creative. Try to observe the Mother Nature like observing the sunset, the patterns of colours like yellow, orange, red and violet.

Observe greenery around, the flora and fauna. Next put your ears and mouth to use and try increasing the observation power. This can be done by walking around the neighbourhood or nearby park and trying to observer new things every day at the same location. Just seeing a thing is not enough, analyse the expressions of the people around you and analyse the emotions they depict. The brain can be fed with many things at once, so carry a camera along and take a lot of pictures of objects from different angles and lighting.

Try to understand and capture the mood and things, which will help in creating a perfect scene. Like vanilla ice-cream will becomes more attractive when cherry and mint leave are added as topping. Play around with the lightning effects.

Take notes along with the pictures. It is like creating a blueprint that will be useful in future works. Things that are important can be underlined or marked with a star.

During this procedure if any question arises in your mind, note them down also, so as to find an answer for them at a later stage. This is a great learning technique. Try to listen a lot, compile those things in brain and then output it through your mind.

Try to create a rhythm between works, something like poetry, but not exactly it. The fifth sense, touch can be used to learn a different perspective of life. Try closing your eyes and feel objects around you like the feel of a satin sheet is more tempting than a cotton sheet.

Develop a habit of carrying a pen and notepad all the time. It is not only useful for taking down notes, but also it can be used as a reminder of meetings and interviews. While waiting for something or someone, scribble on your notepad.

Try to draw things and apply those amazing ideas which come to mind. Go back home and then paint those ideas, if not every day, at least on weekends. Other than painting, try doing something new on weekends like golfing, canoeing, or rock climbing. Watching television and shopping can also provide good ideas.

When something is troubling the mind, do not go to sleep until the issue is resolved. This increases the enthusiasm and determination. Again, note down points in the notepad at this time.

If there is ample time available, join courses that increase creativity like photography, painting, martial arts, etc. It need not be necessary that they be directly linked to advertising. Maintain a diary and note down daily happening, especially good things. Learn the art of humour, read books, watch people and animals, and then apply it practically by trying to put a smile on faces around you.

Do research about great personalities who are related to arts. Read their biographies, some of the problems you are facing may be answered and the path to be taken can be learned.

After going through all the above steps, the creative instincts will start to develop. So, the next time any idea clicks, trust your instincts and work on it. Do not hesitate to try new ideas. And try to interact with people who encourage you with this and believe in you and not inhibit your thinking.

After breaking core, you can approach newspapers, ad agencies with your stories, articles, and original work. Whatever being learnt during the whole experience, there is no harm in sharing and teaching that with others.

Chapter 2

How to Write Good Advertising Content?

To write successful advertisement content is to catch the attention of the customer at first sight as they flicker though the brochures and fliers like they flip through a magazine and not how they will read books with concentration.

It need not be necessary that the customer reads each and every line of the advertisement; hence, each line should be effective and should pass out a message. So, it is not only necessary to write logical matter, but it should also be creative enough.

Firstly, only relevant, and specific matter should be written in the ad. Some content writers fear missing out information and write as much as they can. This will only disinterest customers more and space will be wasted.

The writing style should be related to the type of flier or brochure that is to be written. Its usual for the reader to read skipping lines in between and there is a possibility that they will read it from bottom to top. It always helps to use words that sell. But still, the content should be properly organized with the heading at the top, body in the middle and conclusion at the end. The main points can be written as sub-headings, in bold font.

The body following the sub-heading should discuss the sub-heading and if it is related to any other sub-heading, even those points should be discussed. If the product is to be discussed from the technical point, it should not be so technical that it sounds like a foreign language to a common man.

Chucking is another technique that can be used. Chucking is writing small stories with conclusion at the end. They can either have or not have connection between themselves. Its better if they are not connected, because it will not require the reader to go back to a previous chunk in order to understand the present chunk he is reading.

This works quite well when there are pictures in the advertisement and the chunk illustrates the picture. The two-dimensional picture is speechless unless some well-chosen words talk about it and motivates the customers.

Obviously, while chucking, sub-headings can be used to let out critical information. Another point to be considered is the product or company about which the content is based on. Suppose if the brochure is related to a corporate, the style of writing should be formal.

Spelling mistakes should be avoided to the maximum extent. They reflect poor quality and bring bad reputation to the client. The design should speak clearly and loudly about the organization being discussed.

Unclear, cluttered, and illogical information creates an illusion that the company also has the same characteristics. Catalogues are the only source of advertisement for some businesses, because of low investments. Such kind of business catalogues will not require much writing, just product description will do. Instead, one can work on the font sizes, colours, etc.

The next step should be writing information about contacts so as to buy the product; detailed forms are big turn-off. Contact information, postal address and website URL should be clearly specified. Also include whether the business accepts cash, check or credit card.

Another thing to be taken care of is the contact information, which is usually written on the forms, which have to be mailed. It is better to write them on the advertisement also so that the customers can save it for future reference.

After the final content is written, it is the time for organizing it. Depending on the demand of the products, arrange them in hierarchy, especially when designing a catalogue because each of the products should get the consideration and attention they deserve.

It is a good habit to write down procedures, which have been applied to every kind of advertisements written. And also save the information like what customers were targeted with what kind of advertisements, to use to the same kind of logic the next time to similar customers. This helps to create a blueprint for a future job.

Advertising Using Power Words

Word cannot only influence the minds of people but can completely change their perception abut a particular thing. Words have the persuasion power to entice and motivate.

They are used by the politicians, public relations personals, and even by parents to pass on their message. These words are known as power words and they can do wonders when used in advertisement.

New or improved words create a sense of curiosity. The customers get an impression that the product is something that is different from others and he tries to get it before anyone else does so as to have edge over others.

The laundry products have always been advertised as new and improved, from years. Although it can be either new improved version of the existing product, but the power of both the words and the product reinforces each other's strength.

Take for instance the line 'Money back guarantee', these power words help gain the trust of the customer. It is a must to print these words at the closing line of an advertisement. After this sentence, the methods of payment and how money will be returned if the customer is not satisfied should be stated.

Most of the successful advertisements have a little-known secret that surely generated curiosity within the reader. People are knowledge thirsty; they want to know what others do not know. They think that there is some vital information they are missing because of which they have not gained success in something particular. Words 'Insider say that', is similar to 'secret'. It gives out information from some expertise that is still unknown to the outside world and only if the customer gives money, information will be divulged to him.

Free word in the headline of the message simply does wonders. The reader easily absorbs the message, unless and until something free is given to the customer in reality.

By any change, if the company tricks the customer into paying money for something, which was supposed to be free, the trust of the customer is lost instantly. Usually, the word FREE is spelled as FR~E on websites as ISP filters blocks messages having the actual word, considering it to be some kind of spam.

You are a very important word to be used in an advertisement. It directly points out the advantages to the customer if he buys a particular product or service.

Step into the shoes of the customer and try to note down the points which will be of benefit and what points will decrease the interest. The advantages then should be referred to the customer by addressing them with 'you'. The customer feels that he is being directly talked to. The word 'Immediately' rings in the emergency.

It can be interpreted as 'Don't wait any longer, get it now!' This motivates the customer to take some necessary and quick action.

Power in itself is a powerful word. Give that power to the consumer and see the magic. This gives the consumer a feeling that he can get possession of something that he lacked till now and this could make him achieve the impossible.

The basis of a successful advertisement is to understand the consumer's needs and then design the advertisement accordingly. Just stating the advantages of using the product or service of the company is not enough.

Sentence should be so designed that the customer should see his advantage in the product. For example, when advertising for a digital camera, just stating that the in-built memory of the camera is of 1 GB, will not do the trick.

Instead, the sentence should be changed to 'enough memory to store 350 pictures or 50 videos. The solution to the problem of the customer is reflected in this sentence. Ideas can be taken from advertisements of other similar brands like how the sentences are written and placed in an advertisement.

After the sentence framing, adding power words to spice up the advertisement will definitely make a winning ad campaign.

Chapter 3

Characteristics of a Successful Advertisement

Many small businesses don't get success they want from advertising due to availability of very little resources.

The results are simply flat due to lack of good ideas for improvements. Whether the ads are put in a local newspaper or are printed in the famous periodical or posted on a website, the money invested should gain the desired outcome. There are some common mistakes small businesses and professional service providers do when designing, posting advertisement, which leads to the failure of the advertisement.

Bigger is better is believed in by many. That is exactly what some of the small firms think when they want to advertise their product. They think bigger and select a medium where they need to invest a lot of money, but do not reach targeted market.

Like if a company specializes in designing diet plans and want to help out people who had disappointing results from their individual diet plans, and the company chooses to advertise a full page in the local paper instead of running advertisement in a health magazine, obviously not many of the dieters will notice the advertisement and the advertisement does not get the desired attention.

So, the point is to come up with the best campaign, which will increase the probability of the ad getting viewed and the right customers trying to buy the product or sign up for the service.

Studies and research can be carried out on the market and targeted audience can be narrowed down. Once getting the list of newspapers, magazines and magazines meant for the customers in mind, find out how many readers they have and the cost they ask for posting the ad. Special deals are offered by them from time to time and can only be found by watchful eye.

It is estimated that everyday people are subjected to around three thousand commercials. That is a huge number and if someone desires to be noticed, he should certainly be different. Not only the services and product sold should be unique in the market, so should be the advertisement.

For example, if a business selling mattresses says, "We sell mattresses", it will not make a statement and will be passed off as any other mattress advertisement.

But if they say, "Our mattresses are of the finest quality", it will make the advertisement stand out in the crowd.

Other catch lines are "Are you suffering from back pain? Probably you must try our mattresses," are more specific and will catch the fancy of the people who are suffering from back pains since a long time. The advertisement should also focus on the uniqueness of the product and how it is better compared to the competitors' product.

Focusing on the problems of the customers and giving a solution for them, is what a customer demand. A customer does not buy a product; he buys benefits in the form of a product.

The real value of the product should be realized and a clear picture of it should be presented to the customer, so he will be able to relate with the product. If the advertisement does not specify the solution it can provide, the customers will never know of it. So, focusing on the customers problem is what some ads miss.

The last thing missing in most of the advertisement is motivation for the customers. If the advertiser has designed the advertisement and the customer had read the advertisement, all efforts and money invested will be wasted if he does not get up and do something about it.

It should not be assumed that the customer knows what to do; instead, the advertisement should influence the mind of the customer and should tell him what to do. Call of action is the final job of the advertisement.

It should call for information or visiting the store or even visiting the online store. The message should sound confident and clear.

Research in Advertising

Research in advertising is done in order to produce better advertisements that are more efficient in motivating customers to buy a product or a service.

The research can be based on a particular advertising campaign or can be more generalized and based on how advertisements create an effect on people's mind. Lots of approaches are involved to go about conducting an advertising research like economical, psychological, demographical, and sociological.

When designing an advertisement for a particular product many things should be researched like where it should be displayed, whether the advertisement can be printed in newspapers or magazines or broadcasted on television or radio or published on the Internet.

Many methods are undertaken to collect relevant information. The research itself is of two kinds, syndicated and customized. Syndicated research is a single research done by the company that is available to other companies as well.

Customized research is research based on certain criteria and is done for a particular company and its results are available to only that company.

Pre-testing or copy testing is a type of customized research that determines the in-market efficiency of an advertisement before it is released or before the final production. The more the pre-testing is done the more likely that it will be a successful advertisement and each pre-testing should be applied number of times.

This can be done by studying the level of attention the customers have, motivation, brand linkage, communication, and entertainment. Flow of emotions and flow of attention are broken down and studied individually. The results are applied on the advertisement that is still being developed to recognize the weak points and replace them.

A reliable feedback loop can guide researchers, client, and the agency to work in harmony. Tests should be applied during the storyboard stage of ad making. This is an early stage, and the results are highly predictive. During this process images are selected and used as integrated campaign print ad.

Post-testing or ad tracking studies are either syndicated or customized. Studies are done over a period of time or continuously. The in-market research is done to understand a brands linkage, performance, awareness, and preference along with product attitudes and usage.

They are done by, conducting interviews either on phone or Internet. Testing finished advertisement provides confidence and gives an idea whether it is following the strategy.

All the above studies should facilitate client's advertisement development make the end product easier to achieve.

Study should contain rational information having not only surface knowledge but also provide deep in-sight that will open window to a customer's mind.

The customer, too, should provide precise information based on facts and not based on imaginary thinking and self-delusion. He should be able to explain the role of advertisement in the whole marketing plan. Working in vacuum does not get the desired result.

The basis is to provide in-depth understanding about the consumers for improving on the advertisement techniques and other marketing decisions.

The traditional methods of qualitative and quantitative techniques have been improved to analyse information with good insight.

The rapidly changing likes and needs of the customers are difficult to track but should be studied in order to increase the quality of advertisement. The changes are because of the huge number of options offered to them by the market.

Chapter 4

Advertising for Free

Advertising for free seems like an impossible thing when heard.

But there are several ways by which the cost of advertisement can be conserved, with the help of some imagination and creativity.

A business wanting to advertise, can write articles related to their field of expertise that can be submitted to media and publications having interest in that particular field. The advertising article can have information about the company and dealership opportunity.

Due to the rise in Internet users and websites, new websites have sprung up which offer free services. Articles can be written for these websites and they can be broadcasted for free, which will be viewed by hundreds of people every day.

Once the business has gained some recognition, within no time it will gain popularity also among the crowds. This popularity can lead to them being invited on radio and television talk shows and even to interviews.

Such kind of opportunities should not be missed as they provide a chance for free promotion. If it is taking a long time to get a break, the producer can be addressed with a letter that can be followed up by a telephone call or in-person visit.

During the visit, the nature of expertise can be discussed about the business, which will be of interest to the viewers of the particular channel. Once a businessperson gains the status of being public-friendly, more offers start pouring in.

Free bulletin board located in the neighbourhood, like in grocery stores, libraries, and salons, are another good idea. Advertising circulars can be posted on such boards for free.

Circulars for mass distribution can be handed out at the mall, shopping centre, bus stops, particularly on weekends when there is a big rush. Students can be hired on part time basis for this purpose.

Promotional advertisement can be printed on the envelopes used by the business firms. Both the sender and the receiver can view this advertisement. Promotional offers can be sent to customers by postcards, which should be utilized to its full, leaving only place left for writing the address.

Some of the new mail order publications offer free first time and seasonal deductions for advertisers. Other publications offer pay per inquiry space.

Inquiries can be made about stand-by space, which means that the publication holds the submission of advertisement until the space is not sold and, in that case, thirty three percent saving can be achieved. Usually, local newspapers provide these kinds of offers.

If the business is involved in ad sheet or catalog publishing, other publishers can be contacted for the purpose of bartering an advertising exchange. They can place advertisement in their publication, in return for placing their advertisement in the business's publication.

Free offers can be provided to the customer. This can be done by emailing or printing newsletter about information regarding the area of interest of the targeted customers and can be made popular by using tag lines. Attach a free coupon with it, which the customers can use it for shopping, if a criterion is met like minimum purchase of $ 50. By this the response will be huge and most of them will purchase something or the other to avail the free offer.

The basic ingredient for advertising for free is imagination and research. Opportunities should be searched, and a strong working force should be applied to increase the sales.

Search Engine Optimization and Advertising

In today's net-savvy world it has become common for any business to have a website which they use mostly for advertising their products and services.

With the advent of search engines, it has become even easier for the customers to search for the stuff online. For a website to be successful its link should land in the first three pages which the search engine brings, and the rank of the page should be high which means many visitors come to the site.

This can be achieved by applying search engine optimization or popularly known as SEO. This is a marketing strategy which increases the quality and quantity of traffic flow to a particular website via search engines.

SEO not only affects the search engine results, but also image search, video search and industry specific vertical search engines. It determines how a search algorithm functions and searches what is popular with people.

When a website link is submitted to a search engine, a spider crawls through a page to gather links which lead to other pages and stores those pages on the server of the search engine.

The information collected from these pages is sent to the indexer, whose job is to extract information from those pages such as the keywords and their weights, the location of page and other links that are stored for the spider to crawl in future.

In the beginning, the search engine optimizer algorithms were dependent on the keywords, Meta tags, and index files provided by the Webmaster.

Meta tags provided information about a particular page but using them for indexing the pages did not prove to be successful as some Webmasters added irrelevant Meta tags to increase the number of hits and earn huge ad revenue.

They even changed the HTML of the web pages to achieve a good rank for the page. But this was a case of abuse as it fetched irrelevant pages.

Search engines then began utilizing complex ranking algorithm, which were difficult for the webmasters to manipulate so as to provide web surfers with genuine results. The rank of the web page was calculated mathematically by functions using strength and quantity of the inbound links.

The higher the rank of the page the more chances it had to be viewed by a person. Later algorithms were developed which considered various other on-page factors such as rank and off-page factors such as hyperlink.

Since the webmasters could not manipulate the page rank, they began exchanging, selling and buying links, which lead to link spamming and even creation of numerous sites dedicated for this purpose.

Algorithms became more complex by every passing day and top search engines kept their algorithms a secret. As the cost of SEO increased, advertisers were roped in to pay for it, which finally resulted in high quality web pages.

Although investing in SEO is very fruitful, but at the same time is risky because without any prior notice the algorithms being used are bound to change and the search engine will stop directing visitors to the page. Many consultants are available in the market that provides SEO services.

They manipulate the HTML source code of the web site like menus, shopping carts and sometimes even the content of the website to draw more traffic.

Search engines like Yahoo has algorithms that extract pages not according to the page rank but according to the cost per click or set fee, that is if an advertiser desires that the page containing his ad be displayed, he is expected to pay money for it.

This is a point of controversy, as only the big businesses will be able to increase the number of hits of their page but not the small business who might be having a better-quality page.

Google Ad Words explores ads which have words typed in the search box by the surfer. The Million Dollar Homepage started the concept of Pixel advertising, which is a graphical kind of advertising.

Depending on the pixels, the space is sold to the advertiser. Keyword advertising involves advertisers who buy URLs of a site and place their ads at that location. Thus, SEO is a market in its own which is yielding great results for businesses on Internet.

Chapter 5

Writing A Good Headline for Your Advertisement

A dvertisements of products, organizations, and services are generally aired on television. This is be done by buying slots on the airtime from a particular television channel. Price depends on the popularity of the channel, time the commercial is being aired, number of viewers and length of the commercial.

Placing a commercial on local channels is more affordable than on national channel where the cost is almost double. When thinking of placing a commercial on television it is advised that you first understand what audience needs to be reached.

Different audiences have different taste, which can be determined by their choice of television show like celebrity talk, cartoons, sports, reality, news, movies, soaps, prime time etc.

Prime time is usually Advertising Your Business 29 from 6 to 7 pm and is the most expensive slot. Following it is the news time at noon or 10-11 pm slots, which are proven to be the most effective time slots for the success of a commercial. More affordable is the 12-4 pm soap time.

Always check out with the sales representative for the prices. When advertising on national level, check out an ad agency that usually works on commission basis. It is highly recommended to negotiate during a re-run of the advertisement and stay away from paying the complete amount.

Compare the prices of different networks and different programs before you place an ad. Another money saving trick is to buy a thirty seconds slot and air commercials of ten to fifteen seconds of length one after the other.

This increases the possibility of target viewers seeing the commercial without the cost of re-runs. But this is risky as the pressure of conveying critical information in a short period of time increases. So, the commercials should not be so short that the actual message could not be delivered correctly to the audience. Usually, a reminder commercial can be of a shorter duration.

Look out for the people who would like to buy a slot that has already been purchased. This can be very tricky as it will be more like a bid for which they will be ready to pay a larger amount sometimes even double because they badly need a slot.

This usually happens during the holiday season, which comes in the last quarter of the year around New Year's Eve, Thanksgiving holidays and Christmas holidays. Best time of the year to buy slots for commercial is the first and second quarter of the year.

Price is usually negotiable during the first quarter as the sales representatives give discounts to advertisers who have spent a lot of money advertising during the holiday season and are trying to recover from it.

If planning to pay for advertising commercials for the whole year check out the discounts that are being offered for advertising round the year. Usually, a five percent discount is offered when signing for a six-month time period and ten percent when signing for a twelve-month time period.

But do keep in mind to check out exactly when the commercials are being aired because these discounts are usually offered to distract people from this point and the commercials are aired during odd hours and also not during the holiday season.

The very first commercial to go on air was of Bulova Watch Company on WNBC, United States of America on July 1, 1941. And ever since then there have been no stopping and now commercials sell anything that one can ever imagine.

Chapter 6

Low-Cost Advertising

There is no better advertisement campaign that is low cost and also successful at the same time.

Great business ideas when utilized effectively can save lots of money. This is not only easy for those who work full-time as an advertiser, but also for those who work from home.

Advertising from home is also a low-cost option, which involves making and distributing fliers. Usually, potential customers will visit home for business dealing.

Print good number of fliers and give it to anyone who is visiting home like family, friends, mailman, etc. Business cards can also be distributed. Few selected people can be given sample of the product.

For those who work outside home, employ college students to distribute fliers at supermarkets, community centres, or malls, especially on weekends, when there is a rush.

Spread the word by the mouth. Talk to everyone about the product and ask them to talk about it to others. It is a very powerful tool to increase the network and does not even cost anything.

When receiving a casual call from family members and friends, do not forget to tell them about the latest events, discounts and promotions and ask them about what they are up to. If the parties are into the business, it will not hurt to promote each other. Joint ventures can be started with trustable people of the same trade.

The only cost that will be incurred during the whole process is of printing fliers. For a better quality, professional can be hired to design them, as they will be able to play with colours and write motivating material.

Most of the businesses have company bulletin board that they use to put up company's latest news. Fliers and business cards can be tacked on such bulletin boards. But before doing so, check out with the human resource department before placing the information as most of HR departments make it compulsory to consult them.

Parents are required to be in regular touch with the teachers to know about the progress of the child and they have meetings from time to time. Do not miss this opportunity and spread the word. Hand them the business card and fliers personally at the meeting, instead of just giving the contact number.

Get involved with fundraiser at schools, as it is a nice approach to market business. Prior to handing out the order received, collect all necessary information like business card pack, fliers, with proper information.

Information can be based on what is the company about, what are the products and services provided, or how to get in touch with the company. In each individual order, carefully place all of them and seal the package properly. Presentation, too, is of importance and should be paid attention.

Voice mails can be put to good use, other than recording messages. They can help to deliver the marketing message. Greet with a brief message, following with website and email address, so that whoever calls will be already having telephone number and they will be able to learn more about the business by visiting the website. When the company is providing special promotional offers and discounts, include information about those in the voice mail.

Discontinuation of any services of products can also be informed about. Repetitive voicemails sound boring, so keep changing the voice mail frequently and add some creativity to it.

Most of the big businesses attach business cards or fliers without going mail. This works for companies who send bills to their customers. For those who have customers paying online, they can send the information through emails. Advertisements can be done, in the locality, by placing fliers on bulletin boards of the local grocery stores, businesses, barbers, or butchers.

People frequent these places and there is a possibility of getting a good response. Some businesses place a jar at the reception counter where the business cards can be dropped for future reference, while visiting them.

Advertising on Internet

Ever since the advent of Internet, advertising on the World Wide Web has been very popular. Many corporations, companies and business have taken advantage of this and you can see ads on any web pages you visit.

Consumer can go to any search engine and type the keyword relating to what they are looking for and hit search and they will be provided with a huge list from which they can select. This is a very cost effective and time saving method of advertising. It has become really easy for any business to have a personalized website by which they can advertise, directly interact with the customer; provide details about their product and services. Regular newsletters, offers, discounts can be pasted on site to increase the interest of the website visitors.

Since it is easy to reach any kind of audience concerning any kind of business, the possibility of misuse is always there. Based on this Internet advertising is classified into 2 kinds of advertisement, legal online advertising, and the illegal online advertising.

The Legal online advertising includes online advertising directories, search engine advertising, and e-mail advertising, desktop advertising.

The Illegal advertising is more commonly known as spamming. This is usually done by altering some system settings with the help of external applications after which pop-ups are sent to a particular network or computer.

The external applications are known as adware or spyware. Some of these are really harmful, the most famous being Trojans, which are very hard to uninstall and remove from the system.

With the increase in technology, special effects are being used to make advertisement more interesting. Vivid colours, good page layout and lots of imagination is involved.

Typically, Adobe Flash is used to design advertisements these days. Depending on the technology being used to design advertisements can be classified into various categories.

Banner ads are animations displayed on the website usually created in HTML or Eudora. There is a range of type and sizes of the ads.

Trick banner ads are banner ads that have an extra functionality of dialog boxes and buttons and are displayed as an alert or error message.

A pop-up is an advertisement displayed in a new window that covers up the active web page. A pop-under advertisement opens in another window that is under the active web page and can be seen after present window is either closed or minimized.

Interstitial ads are those that are displayed before directing over to the desired page.

❖ Wallpaper ads form the background of the web page.

❖ The ads that float on the screen are known as a floating ad.

❖ Polite ads download on a low pace without interrupting the normal functioning of the website.

❖ An ad that enlarges and changes the contents of the page being displayed is known as expanding ad.

❖ Advertisements which are displayed in a video form on a website is known as a video ad.

There are many ways by which advertising slots can be purchased on Internet like CPM, CPV, CPC, CPA, CPL and CPO. CPM or cost per mil means that the advertiser is meant to pay for a particular number of people to whom the advertisement will be exposed.

CPV or cost per visitor means that the advertiser is meant to pay for the people to whom the advertisement was delivered. CPC or cost per click means paying for the number of clicks made on the advertisement by the visitors.

Although the advertisement is put up on the website, the amount is paid only after the visitor clicks on the URL of the advertisement.

CPA or cost per action means that the advertisement publisher bares all the charges of advertisement, but he gets paid only if the visitor clicks on the advertisement and purchases a product or signs-up for a service.

CPL or cost per lead is similar to CPA, only that visitor does not have to necessarily buy anything; he or she can simply apply to get regular newsletters and special offers. CPO or cost per order is where the advertiser pays each time an order is placed.

Online advertisements cannot only be used to promote a product or service but in fact they can be used for purposes like promoting charity and spreading education.

Chapter 7

How to Write Business-To-Business Advertisement

Business-to-business firms are those firms that sell products and services among themselves.

Selling is done to a client of other company, who might use product for intermediate purposes or so. Advertisements relating to B2B companies should not only generate interest, but it should also be simply outstanding despite the tough competition.

In the market, there are several firms who produce the same stuff, and they reach out for clients with whom they want to do business. So, finding the right client is not a big deal, but actually getting hold of them is.

In written content, use the name of the company in the first sentence; preferably first word. It is not pleasing to start with "us". Following it, give a brief introduction about the company. In today's busy world people do not have time to waste so deliver the message right away.

Using catchy adjectives will do the trick. The sentence should be framed so that the client knows about the company, what it does and how it is unique from others.

Pose questions before creating the writing material, like what is that the customer will expect, and do they demand high quality. Do not hesitate to use 'you' very often. The reader will feel that he is directly being referenced and it will be easier for him to relate to.

Play with customer's psychology. Understand the difficulties faced by them and then show them how the company or the company's product can solve it. Call of action can be given then and offer to clear their doubts. It should be more than just a helpline. The action should be really immediate. Simply do not let the client slip away. After the initial writing, write in detail about the product or service provided.

This is in-dept information for those concerned about your company's product. Point out the advantages of using them. Write them in a hierarchical form with numbering or bullets. If writing short paragraphs, strong sub-titles can be used as heading of individual paragraphs. Again, using adjectives will be good.

A good amount of entertainment factor should be added. This will retain the interest of the customer and will not distract him. But if lots of it is used, it will simply become shabby. It is a nice idea to use product noun as a verb along with other adjectives.

Submit website and advertisements to search engines. Millions of people use it every day to find what they need. If the website is search engine optimized, it will surely get lots of traffic. The name of the company and keywords should densely populate the website content.

Make it a compulsion for the visitor to go through the advertisement before moving on to the registration or payment process. Some B2B websites do not allow adding an email address or URL in the advertisement. They can be tracked in by actually spelling out dot or at in the email address or website link.

Once the customer is lured, they should be maintained. Product should be delivered on time. Quality should be maintained. Once it is done, not only will they start trusting the company but also at the same time they will spread the word about the company. They will advertise for free. Their experience with the company will motivate others to join the bandwagon.

Impact of Colours in Advertisements

Human brain receives signals faster through eyes rather than ears. Visual appearance is supposed to be more appealing when compared to any other senses, no matter what the medium of presentation is.

So, there are methods by which one can increase the visual appeal. Other senses facilitate visual appeal and are also important to concentrate on.

Typical example is colour when accompanied with audio, and writing. According to a study, big budget companies spend billions in the colour market research, which helps in product and packaging development.

Colour, along with content, helps to pertain the interest of the visitor and makes him surf the website longer. A colourful article will make the reader read it till the end. Colour makes things look more amiable. Colours are known to influence the behaviour of a person. Like blue colour is said to have a relaxing effect. Red represents passion and love. A dating website can have red as the background colour.

Fast food restaurants have bright picture of food beautifully decorated pasted on the walls. This tempts the taste buds of the customer and the customer pounces on the food, eats and leaves quickly. And this is exactly the reaction expected.

Light effects can also be used to play with the mind of the on-looker. Advertisements, especially for food products, have strategically placed lights.

The light effects trigger the hormones in the brain, which increases the hunger. If the same is placed in a slightly dim light, it will not be equally tempting.

Countries around the world have different cultures that relate a colour to an occasion or emotion. Climatic conditions also attribute to this.

Like in America, people relate black to death and whereas in Asia, white is related to death. People living near the equator like warm colours and people living nearer to the poles like cold colours.

It is a must for an advertiser to have the knowledge about the colours and what they refer too. Black stands for elegance, sophistication, seduction, and mystery. White stands for peace, pure, clean, mild, and youthful. Gold stands for prestige, luxury and elite. Silver stands for prestige, scientific and cold. Yellow stands for warmth, happiness, and cheer.

Orange stands for warmth, playfulness, and vibrant. Red stands for love, excitement, strength, passion, and danger. Pink stands for nurture, sweet, soft, and security.

Green stands for nature, fresh, fertility and abundance. Blue stands for cool, trust, belonging and reliability. And lastly Purple stands for spiritual, royalty, and dignity.

From the advertiser's point of view, we can conclude that colours can determine the shopping habits of customers. Black, blue, red and orange attract impulsive buyers. Smart shoppers are attracted to pink, light blue and navy-blue colours.

Companies use colours in logo, advertisement, etc., to pass the right message to the customer. Wal-Mart advertise has a navy-blue background and its catch line is "We sell for less", which means smart customers are their goal. Mercedes has a silver logo, true to its class. Before designing an advertisement, the targeted customers should be recognized, and advertisers should not use the colours that are their personal favourites but according to the ad campaign.

Advertisement for children should have bright and vibrant colours. Yellow, red, blue, green, which are the primary colours, are the colours, which attract the children, which is why parents buy those colours for their kids.

These colours represent warmth, sweetness, trust, reliability, playfulness, and security.

Advertising: Self Promotion

Self-promotion is similar to spreading the word by any other means but with an artistic approach. If the artistic part were taken out of the equation advertising would look more like barging rather than self-promotion.

There are many steps involved in this process. The first step is to collect and create useful content relating to the topic, which is a not an easy job.

In today's fast paced world owning a website for your business is a must which is not a big deal anymore with so many people available who excel in web designing and also offer a competitive rate.

There are many types of technologies involved in the creation of a website, a one-page flash website would not take you places. Intense graphics should be incorporated to catch the eye of the customer. After the creation of website, the website content should be emphasized upon. Writers who expertise in search engine optimization should be raked in so that the page ranks amongst the top pages on Google, Yahoo and Msn.

Search engines have become popular universally and your website doing good on them plays a more vital role than getting other kind of references. Hence, efforts should be made on making remarkable progress to bring your website in the hit list.

Also, material on the website should be updated frequently to meet the changing needs of the people. Get someone to design a logo for the company and website which is catchy and delivers the right message to the customers.

Other than website content, articles should also be published in newspapers, magazines and online publications especially business-oriented emphasizing on ten strong points which describes the best about the business or the product. Online publication will facilitate in providing successful searches to the targeted audience.

The next target method of advertising should be television. Putting a commercial during the prime time will spread the message to a larger crowd.

The content of the advertising should be akin to the value of the product. Famous personalities can be roped in to endorse the product, which will not only attract common people but also their fans in buying the product.

From time to time, it is essential to review the past work and improving on the mistakes previously committed. Once the previous mistakes are tackled, it would not hurt to analyse previous milestones, awards, and acquisitions. This increases the chances of running into something that really deserves to be highlighted to the public. The more accomplishments you display to the public the more fan-following your product will get.

Reviewing competitor's work on a regular basis would prove fruitful. This would also help identify loopholes in your product that have been overlooked before and would provide the key reasons to improve on.

Although this is an old approach, snail mails are also one of the best advertising methods. As it is a more energy consuming approach, it is important that you have the addresses of the customers who are really in need of the product.

Regular mails containing details about the new development will keep people informed about your company's products. A more modern approach to this method is collecting e-mail ids of the targeted customers and posting them ads and latest deals. This is a cheaper and less time-consuming approach compared to snail mails as you can mass email as many people as you want at any time.

Before releasing any product in the market, product testing should be done by giving out samples among the targeted customers. The feedbacks make it clearer whether the product is ready to be released in market or whether changes should be made to make it more appealing to the public.

It is recommended to approach sincere friends, acquaintances, partners, and clients at first to test your product and then go to the public, as expert advice is more useful.

To make more brownie points, address customers and clients and appreciate them for their contribution in making product popular.

Send a token of thanks on special occasions like festivals or on accomplishing an important task.

Customers can also be thanked by offering special discounts and free gifts. After gaining popularity focus should be on retaining the reputation rather than taking things for granted.

Chapter 8

Other Advertising Options

Advergaming: Advertising Through Video Games

The practice of using video games to promote a particular product or an organization is known as "Advergaming". Wired magazine first used this term in a column to describe the commissioning of free online games by large companies, in 2001.

There are 3 categories of Advergaming: ATL Advergaming, BTL Advergaming and TTL Advergaming.

ATL Advergaming can be vaguely explained as a promotional video game. The business incorporates interactive video games on their website so as to create more awareness about their product among the website visitors. This method is also used to attract more visitors to the site and to increase the traffic flow on the website. If the games are made for product advertising, the product is highlighted in the game.

Before the invention of the internet, floppy disks and later compact disks were used as a medium to promote games and in turn a particular product. It started with floppy disk basically to create awareness as well as product promotion. The first Advergame was distributed by American Home Food, which was developed by Chef Boyardee. Taco Bell and Coca Cola followed it by giving customers floppy disks containing promotional games. The first Advergame to be distributed on compact disk was by Chex and General Mill. The graphics of these games have matured from arcade style flash to three-dimensional.

BTL Advergaming comprises of recruitment tools like In-game advertising, militiamen, and edutainment. Usually, the mascot of the particular company is depicted as the hero in such games. Pepsi man and Burger man were the mascots used in promotional games designed by Pepsi and Burger King, respectively. The storyline of these games can be commercial, educational, or political like the game American Army created to attract more youth towards devoting their life to army and also games meant to promote sports like Formula One racing are also a part of this technique.

In-game advertising is more commercial type and is purely targeted for promotion of the product via the game. This is really picking up and even movies are promoted by this method. Like on the website of the movie, The Mummy, there are games which have a storyline similar to the movie and the player is given knowledge of the facts about the movie and its subject, Egyptian Mummy. Educational Advergaming refers to games that portray a moral message to the players.

These games can also act as a medium of advertisement themselves like in the video game of EA Sports, banners of Pepsi line frame of the game. By using this strategy, the companies are able to provide low price or free games to the consumers. This is also effective in reducing the price of games that have a monthly fee.

TTL Advergaming or through the line Advergaming is the rarest form of Advergaming. URL links are embedded into a game that takes the players to the web pages, which has BTL Advergaming. Different methods are used to attract the player to a particular webpage. In the game "Enter the Matrix" URL hyperlinks are depicted in the background, which the player is forced to click to learn about the facts relating to the plot of the next level and at the same time advertises about the product. The curiosity to learn about the theme of the game attracts the player, although it might not be necessary to click to finish the game. Such kinds of games are usually known as link-chases as one link will lead to another. Website visitors are sometimes tempted with a prize to prompt them to click the URL.

This technique of advertising is really beneficial as it not only creates awareness among the player but also among his friends who lands the website upon friend's suggestion. The success of Advergaming is dependent on word of mouth and thus is also known as viral marketing.

In the year 2004, this industry generated around $83.6 million and involved 105 million players.

Advertising for Free

Advertising for free seems like an impossible thing when heard. But there are several ways by which the cost of advertisement can be conserved, with the help of some imagination and creativity.

A business wanting to advertise, can write articles related to their field of expertise that can be submitted to media and publications having interest in that particular field. The advertising article can have information about the company and dealership opportunity. Due to the rise in Internet users and websites, new websites have sprung up which offer free services. Articles can be written for these websites and they can be broadcasted for free, which will be viewed by hundreds of people every day.

Once the business has gained some recognition, within no time it will gain popularity also among the crowds. This popularity can lead to them being invited on radio, television talk shows and even to interviews.

Such kind of opportunities should not be missed as they provide a chance for free promotion. If it is taking a long time to get a break, the producer can be addressed with a letter that can be followed up by a telephone call or in-person visit. During the visit, the nature of expertise can be discussed about the business, which will be of interest to the viewers of particular channel. Once a businessperson gains status of being public-friendly, more offers start pouring in.

Free bulletin board located in the neighbourhood, like in grocery stores, libraries, and salons, are another good idea. Advertising circulars can be posted on such boards for free. Circulars for mass distribution can be handed out at the mall, shopping centre, bus stops, particularly on weekends when there is a big rush. Students can be hired on part time basis for this purpose.

Promotional advertisement can be printed on the envelopes used by the business firms. Both the sender and the receiver can view this advertisement. Promotional offers can be sent to customers by postcards, which should be utilized to its full, leaving only place left for writing the address.

Some of the new mail order publications offer free first time and seasonal deductions for advertisers. Other publications offer pay per inquiry space. Inquiries can be made about stand-by space, which means that publication holds the submission of advertisement until the space is not sold and, in that case, thirty three percent saving can be achieved.

Usually, local newspapers provide these kinds of offers. If the business is involved in ad sheet or catalog publishing, other publishers can be contacted for the purpose of bartering an advertising exchange. They can place advertisement in their publication, in return for placing their advertisement in the business's publication.

Free offers can be provided to the customer. This can be done by emailing or printing newsletter about information regarding the area of interest of the targeted customers and can be made popular by using tag lines. Attach a free coupon with it, which the customers can use it for shopping, if a criterion is met like minimum purchase of $ 50. By this the response will be huge and most of them will purchase something or the other to avail the free offer.

The basic ingredient for advertising for free is imagination and research. Opportunities should be searched, and a strong working force should be applied to increase the sales.

Advertising in Yellow Pages

Some people believe that yellow pages do not receive response like other advertising methods do and this is true to some extent but not in totality. When talking about traditional yellow pages, there sure is a decline in number of people opting for advertising in it. According to a recent report, even the most attractive advertisement in a particular section is not getting the response from callers like they used to get before. On the contrary, the prices of placing ads in directories are on a rise, which speaks a different, story altogether.

In reality different categories are witnessing different rates of decline. Like the lawyers category is seeing the maximum decline, whereas emergency service provider's section has the same call rate. And sections like mobile phones, real estate and furniture are seeing a rise due to the increasing customer demand. Altering the size of the advertisement or changing the look cannot do wonders any more.

Experts suggest that relying on yellow pages to get customers is not enough. Other options should be considered as well along with it. With the Internet reaching every home, nearly half of the Internet users use the net every day. They prefer to buy stuff online, from the comfort of their homes. Research should be done on the Internet to get reviews about the product. People, who do not usually shop online, also are also opting to shop online as information is provided at the click of a mouse. It is easier for people to trust as customers who used the product give their feedback about the product after using it.

A relatively newer concept is the yellow pages going online. The good thing about them is that they are updated frequently unlike the printed directories and can be viewed from any part of the world.

According to researchers conducted, the response increased by twenty five percent every year. So those who are interested to invest in yellow pages advertising can think of going online. Directories are submitted to search engines, which on typing a keyword or phrase bring the results. Small and local businesses, too, can land on the pages brought by the result. The cost of creating a website can be saved if all the relevant information about the company is included in the online yellow pages. Look out for the date to renew the directory listing, and if there is a need to change the advertisement, it is not a big problem on online yellow pages.

Some starter websites offer to place advertisement in their yellow pages for free. Search out for such websites on the Internet. Larger businesses can start their own websites and place links in the online yellow pages. Articles can be framed about business and can be submitted to Ezines and websites related to the area of business.

Some websites also allow posting articles for free. The purpose of the yellow pages is basically to get potential customers but that does not mean existing customers should be neglected. Steps should be taken to strengthen the relationship with them and to retain their trust by maintaining the standard of the products supplied to them. Once they are completely satisfied, the price-rise will not bother them and they will talk about the company to people they know, which will fetch new customers.

The objective is to work smartly and select the right method of advertising. If a business is not using any other method for advertising apart from using yellow pages, it can cause problems and the products may not sell. Analyse how much money is spent on placing ads in directories and estimate whether number of customers the business gets is desirable. Whenever a call is received from a potential customer, ask them how they got to know about the enterprise. This will help to analyse which advertising method is ideal for the business. It is never late to correct the mistake and go for the right method.

Advertising on Internet

Ever since the advent of Internet, advertising on the World Wide Web has been very popular. Many corporations, companies and business have taken advantage of this and you can see ads on any web pages you visit. Consumer can go to any search engine and type the keyword relating to what they are looking for and hit search and they will be provided with a huge list from which they can select. This is a very cost effective and time saving method of advertising.

It has become really easy for any business to have a personalized website by which they can advertise, directly interact with the customer; provide details about their product and services. Regular newsletters, offers, discounts can be pasted on site to increase the interest of the website visitors.

Since it's easy to reach any kind of audience concerning any kind of business, the possibility of misuse is always there. Based on this Internet advertising is classified into two kinds of advertisement, legal online advertising, and illegal online advertising. Legal online advertising includes online advertising directories, search engine advertising, e-mail advertising, and desktop advertising. Illegal advertising is more commonly known as spamming. This is usually done by altering some system settings with the help of external applications after which pop-ups are sent to a particular network or computer.

The external applications are known as adware or spyware. Some of these are really harmful, the most famous being Trojans, which are very hard to uninstall and remove from the system.

With the increase in technology, special effects are being used to make advertisement more interesting. Vivid colours, good page layout and lots of imagination is involved. Typically, Adobe Flash is used to design advertisements these days. Depending on technology being used to design advertisements can be classified into various categories.

Banner ads are animations displayed on the website usually created in HTML or Eudora. There is a range of type and sizes of the ads. Trick banner ads are banner ads that have an extra functionality of dialog boxes and buttons and are displayed as an alert or error message.

A pop-up is an advertisement displayed in a new window that covers up the active web page. A pop-under advertisement opens in another window that is under the active web page and can be seen after the present window is either closed or minimized.

Interstitial ads are those that are displayed before directing over to the desired page. Wallpaper ads form the background of the web page. The ads that float on the screen are known as a floating ad.

Polite ads download on a low pace without interrupting the normal functioning of the website. An ad that enlarges and changes the contents of the page being displayed is known as expanding ad. Advertisements which are displayed in a video form on a website is known as a video ad.

There are many ways by which advertising slots can be purchased on Internet like CPM, CPV, CPC, CPA, CPL and CPO. CPM or cost per mil means that the advertiser is meant to pay for a particular number of people to whom the advertisement will be exposed.

CPV or cost per visitor means that the advertiser is meant to pay for the people to whom the advertisement was delivered. CPC or cost per click means paying for the number of clicks made on the advertisement by the visitors. Although the advertisement is put up on the website, the amount is paid only after the visitor clicks on the URL of the advertisement. CPA or cost per action means that the advertisement publisher bares all the charges of advertisement, but he gets paid only if the visitor clicks on the advertisement and purchases a product or signs-up for a service. CPL or cost per lead is similar to CPA, only that the visitor does not have to necessarily buy anything; he or she can simply apply to get regular newsletters and special offers. CPO or cost per order is where the advertiser pays each time an order is placed.

Online advertisements cannot only be used to promote a product or service but in fact they can be used for purposes like promoting charity and spreading education.

Advertising on Television

Advertisements of products, organizations, and services are generally aired on television. This is be done by buying slots on the airtime from a particular television channel. Price depends on the popularity of the channel, time the commercial is being aired, number of viewers and length of the commercial.

Placing a commercial on local channels is more affordable than on national channel where the cost is almost double.

When thinking of placing a commercial on television it is advised that you first understand what audience needs to be reached. Different audiences have different taste, which can be determined by their choice of television show like celebrity talk, cartoons, sports, reality, news, movies, soaps, prime time etc. Prime time is usually from 6 to 7 pm and is the most expensive slot. Following it is the news time at noon or 10-11 pm slots, which are proven to be the most effective time slots for the success of a commercial. More affordable is the 12-4 pm soap time. Always check out with the sales representative for the prices. When advertising on national level, check out an ad agency that usually works on commission basis.

It is highly recommended to negotiate during a re-run of the advertisement and stay away from paying the complete amount.

Compare the prices of different networks and different programs before you place an ad. Another money saving trick is to buy a thirty seconds slot and air commercials of ten to fifteen seconds of length one after the other. This increases the possibility of target viewers seeing the commercial without the cost of re-runs. But this is risky as the pressure of conveying critical information in a short period of time increases. So, the commercials should not be so short that the actual message could not be delivered correctly to the audience. Usually, a reminder commercial can be of a shorter duration.

Look out for the people who would like to buy a slot that has already been purchased. This can be very tricky as it will be more like a bid for which they will be ready to pay a larger amount sometimes even double because they badly need a slot. This usually happens during the holiday season, which comes in the last quarter of the year around New Year's Eve, Thanksgiving holidays and Christmas holidays. Best time of the year to buy slots for commercial is the first and second quarter of the year. Price is usually negotiable during the first quarter as the sales representatives give discounts to advertisers who have spent a lot of money advertising during the holiday season and are trying to recover from it.

If planning to pay for advertising commercials for the whole year check out the discounts that are being offered for advertising round the year. Usually, a five percent discount is offered when signing for a six-month time period and ten percent when signing for a twelve-month time period. But do keep in mind to check out exactly when the commercials are being aired because these discounts are usually offered to distract people from this point and the commercials are aired during odd hours and also not during the holiday season.

The very first commercial to go on air was of Bulova Watch Company on WNBC, United States of America on July 1, 1941. And ever since then there have been no stopping and now commercials sell anything that one can ever imagine.

Advertising: Self Promotion

Self-promotion is similar to spreading the word by any other means but with an artistic approach. If the artistic part were taken out of the equation advertising would look more like barging rather than self-promotion. There are many steps involved in this process. The first step is to collect and create useful content relating to the topic, which is a not an easy job.

In today's fast paced world owning a website for your business is a must which is not a big deal anymore with so many people available who excel in web designing and also offer a competitive rate. There are many types of technologies involved in the creation of a website, a one-page flash website would not take you places.

Intense graphics should be incorporated to catch the eye of the customer. After the creation of website, the website content should be emphasized upon. Writers who expertise in search engine optimization should be raked in so that the page ranks amongst the top pages on Google, Yahoo and Msn. Search engines have become popular universally and your website doing good on them plays a more vital role than getting other kind of references. Hence, efforts should be made on making remarkable progress to bring your website in the hit list. Also, material on the website should be updated frequently to meet the changing needs of the people. Get someone to design a logo for the company and website which is catchy and delivers the right message to the customers.

Other than website content, articles should also be published in newspapers, magazines and online publications especially business-oriented emphasizing on 10 strong points which describes the best about the business or the product. Online publication will facilitate in providing successful searches to the targeted audience.

The next target method of advertising should be television. Putting a commercial during the prime time will spread the message to a larger crowd. The content of the advertising should be akin to the value of the product. Famous personalities can be roped in to endorse the product, which will not only attract common people but also their fans in buying the product.

From time to time, it is essential to review the past work and improving on the mistakes previously committed. Once the previous mistakes are tackled, it would not hurt to analyse previous milestones, awards, and acquisitions. This increases the chances of running into something that really deserves to be highlighted to the public. The more accomplishments you display to the public the more fan-following your product will get.

Reviewing competitor's work on a regular basis would prove fruitful. This would also help identify loopholes in your product that have been overlooked before and would provide the key reasons to improve on.

Although this is an old approach, snail mails are also one of the best advertising methods. As it is a more energy consuming approach, it's important that you have the addresses of the customers who are really in need of the product. Regular mails containing details about the new development will keep people informed about your company's products. A more modern approach to this method is collecting e-mail ids of the targeted customers and posting them ads and latest deals. This is a cheaper and less time-consuming approach compared to snail mails as you can mass email as many people as you want at any time.

Before releasing any product in the market, product testing should be done by giving out samples among the targeted customers. The feedbacks make it clearer whether the product is ready to be released in the market or whether changes should be made to make it more appealing to the public.

It is recommended to approach sincere friends, acquaintances, partners, and clients at first to test your product and then go to the public, as expert advice is more useful.

To make more brownie points, address the customers and clients and appreciate them for their contribution in making the product popular. Send a token of thanks on special occasions like festivals or on accomplishing an important task. Customers can also be thanked by offering special discounts and free gifts. After gaining popularity focus should be on retaining the reputation rather than taking things for granted.

Advertising Using Power Words

Word cannot only influence the minds of people but can completely change their perception abut a particular thing. Words have the persuasion power to entice and motivate. They are used by the politicians, public relations personals, and even by parents to pass on their message.

These words are known as power words and they can do wonders when used in advertisement.

New or improved words create a sense of curiosity. The customers get an impression that the product is something that is different from others and he tries to get it before anyone else does so as to have edge over others. The laundry products have always been advertised as new and improved, from years. Although it can be either new improved version of the existing product, but the power of both the words and the product reinforces each other's strength.

Take for instance the line 'Money back guarantee', these power words help gain the trust of the customer. It is a must to print these words at the closing line of an advertisement. After this sentence, the methods of payment and how money will be returned if the customer is not satisfied should be stated.

Most of the successful advertisements have a little-known secret that surely generated curiosity within the reader. People are knowledge thirsty; they want to know what others do not know. They think that there is some vital information they are missing because of which they have not gained success in something particular. Words 'Insider say that', is similar to 'secret'. It gives out information from some expertise that is still unknown to the outside world and only if the customer gives money, information will be divulged to him.

Free word in the headline of the message simply does wonders. The reader easily absorbs the message, unless and until something free is given to the customer in reality. By any change, if the company tricks the customer into paying money for something, which was supposed to be free, the trust of the customer is lost instantly. Usually, the word FREE is spelled as FR~E on websites as ISP filters blocks messages having the actual word, considering it to be some kind of spam.

You are a very important word to be used in an advertisement. It directly points out the advantages to the customer if he buys a particular product or service. Step into the shoes of the customer and try to note down the points which will be of benefit and what points will decrease the interest. The advantages then should be referred to customer by addressing them with 'you'. The customer feels that he is being directly talked to. The word 'Immediately' rings in the emergency. It can be interpreted as 'Don't wait any longer, get it now!' This motivates customer to take some necessary and quick action.

Power in itself is a powerful word. Give that power to the consumer and see the magic. This gives the consumer a feeling that he can get possession of something that he lacked till now and this could make him achieve the impossible.

The basis of a successful advertisement is to understand the consumer's needs and then design the advertisement accordingly. Just stating the advantages of using the product or service of the company is not enough. Sentence should be so designed that the customer should see his advantage in the product. For example, when advertising for a digital camera, just stating that the in-built memory of the camera is of 1 GB, will not do the trick. Instead, the sentence should be changed to 'enough memory to store 350 pictures or 50 videos'. The solution to the problem of the customer is reflected in this sentence. Ideas can be taken from advertisements of other similar brands like how the sentences are written and placed in an advertisement. After the sentence framing, adding power words to spice up the advertisement will definitely make a winning ad campaign.

Billboard Advertising

Outdoor advertising is a low budget and effective way of advertising a company's product. Among the entire methods billboard advertising is the most sort after method, which has been proven to be the best sales strategy in the recent times. Nearly 5.6 billion dollars was spent on billboard advertising alone, in the year 2006, as analysed by Outdoor Advertising Association of America.

Billboard advertising is the best bet in outdoor advertising and is not that costly. And with the amount of exposure the product gets the money is worth it. In the past few years, several factors have triggered billboard advertising and cost effectiveness being one of the prime reasons. One of the reasons being if an ad is placed in the local newspaper or a television channel the advertisement gets noticed for only thirty seconds and when the same advertisement is placed on billboard, it gets noticed throughout the day, for months.

Thousands of people view billboard every day on their way to jobs or home, it does not get lost in the pages like an advertisement placed in a newspaper or magazine. There is a frequent and continuous delivery of message.

No other advertising method can grab the attention of people like billboard advertising. It creates brand awareness and strong name recognition.

One of the reasons behind the cost being low is technology. In the early years, the billboards were hand-painted due to which the labour cost was high. Now, advertisers design and print their advertisements on a huge poster board or vinyl board by a computer-aided printer, which is very cost effective.

Creativity can be achieved to the highest extent, with ease and less money. The brighter, colourful, creative the advertisement is, the more eye-catching it is. With the advancements in technology, it takes very less time to design billboards with unlimited possibilities.

Before placing a billboard advertisement in a particular area, it is better that a research is done about the interest of the people in and around that area. Like if the advertiser desires to post a billboard advertisement on a highway, he can choose the advertisement on a motel, cafeteria, or gas station. Depending on the locality specific potential customers should be targeted.

The cost is really reasonable. It varies from $1,000 to $3,000 per month. Ten advertisements will cost around $ 30,000. It might look like a big amount, but it costs almost same if placing a full-page ad in a newspaper for only a day. And if the effectiveness is considered for both the methods, newspaper advertisements are not even half as effective as billboard advertisements.

When an advertisement is placed in a newspaper or in a magazine, the customer should reach out to see advertisement, but when an advertisement is placed on a billboard, it is like reaching to the customers.

Thus, Billboard advertising has high impact on people and is a cost-effective method of advertisement. The above-mentioned advantages are few of the many advantages of billboard advertising. And that is the reason why all types of companies and businesses are choosing to go with billboard advertising. From placing the billboard at a theatre multiplex, highway, airport, and even pasting them on cars, any kind of product can be advertised to any kind of audience. And the effectiveness of it can never be underestimated.

Celebrity Branding

Celebrity branding is a method of advertising which uses the services of a celebrity to promote a product or service with the help of their fame and status in the society. This method has several approaches; it can involve a celebrity simply appearing in a commercial and the celebrity can be signed for attending events for promotion. Another method is to start a product line using their name as a brand. Perfume and garments are the largest product lines involving such a promotion. All the top actors, singers and models are known to give their name to a certain brand or licensed products. Jennifer Lopez started her own line of clothing a while ago which features designer clothes personally designed by her.

A customer's buying behaviour is hugely influenced by famous people. Marketing experts, using associative learning principles, analyses the lifestyle of the celebrities to properly assign them to the brand which depicts them perfectly. Their fashion sense, appeal, awareness, fame, and public image are reviewed thoroughly to assign them the right charity work or product. Repetition, blocking, CS pre-exposure, extinction, overshadowing, belongingness, and association set size are the principles on the basis of which analysis is done like the famous Miss World Aishwarya Rai of India who has very beautiful eyes was chosen to campaign for eye donation project. Some of the celebrities are known for their distinct voice. This concept led to the voice-over method in advertising. Their voices merely attract customers when used in a commercial.

Today, nearly twenty percent of the advertising industry utilizes celebrity endorsement. A celebrity is bound to endorse many products and brands over a course of time. Each time a different image of the celebrity is being projected to the public. The company should keep in mind the previous identity and play accordingly. Projecting a different person every time will sustain the interest of the customers, but at the same time the two identities should not conflict with each other. The captain of England soccer team David Beckham has endorsed many products. While advertising for Gillette, his taste for hairstyles was considered and he was given a bald look.

When campaigning for Police his passion for fashion was portrayed all over and heavily jewelled David Beckham was depicted.

If a celebrity is not comfortable with being pictured differently each time, he or she can create a graphic image or logo of their own which can be used each time they advertise for a particular product. The logo can reflect the personality of the respective celebrity, like the font can be stylish if the celebrity is fashion conscious like Jennifer Lopez who created a logo of JLO, which is used to advertise perfume and even clothing line of her own. Another advantage in this approach is that the brand can still be appealing to the crowds even after the celebrity has lost his or her looks as they will not require visual recognition and aids in the long-term negotiations. The celebrity logo itself carries the style and attitude.

Millions of dollars are being invested by marketers to get the promotional support of super stars every year. Davie Brown Entertainment has an agency completely devoted to the purpose of choosing a celebrity for a product.

They not only judge a celebrity's calibre to affect brand affinity and consumer's taste but also design the advertisements for the celebrities to feature in it.

Low Budget Advertising

After the advent of online selling sites, shopping has been made so easy that it can be done within the comfort of the home. Online selling gave rise to online advertising also known as iAdvertising, which is proving to be the best way to reach a larger audience within a short time using less money.

There are many options available on the Internet to get started. Creating a website and then placing its link on different websites is one of the ways. Pages can be submitted to the search engines after applying search engine optimization techniques. Websites offer various payment methods. Some take money for simply placing an ad or link on their website, some take money only if a visitor clicks on the link or website and some take money only if the visitors visit a link and have bought something or availed some service. There are options available for the type of ad being placed. There are pop-up ads, banner ads, wallpaper ads, polite ads, video ads, etc. Businesses with really low budget can send mails to targeted customers.

Radio stations offer a good price to advertise during the non-peak time. Get in touch with the local station and try to ask for a discount. The same applies to television; even they have a minimal amount for advertising slots during the non-prime hours, especially after midnight. Contact different television station to compare pricing.

The age-old tradition of advertising in yellow pages directories is always a success. All businesses from small to big register themselves in the yellow pages and have sworn to be benefited from it. People can look up for contact numbers, addresses and services offered directly from the pages.

Newspaper is the next best thing. First analyse the audience to be targeted by age group, sex, and location. Choose the local newspaper and section where ad should be placed depending on the audiences to be targeted. The classifieds department of the local newspapers have special offers, find out in detail about the pricing structure for the size of the advertisements, number of words, font size, etc.

Design the business cards with accuracy. Try to include all the vital information about the business like the name of the company, where it is located, services provided, working hours, and contact information like landline number, cell number and person to be contacted. Personalized business cards are good way of reaching the genuine customers. Other way to advertise is to give presentations on your products. Brochures can be inserted in business presentation package.

Other than things like history of company and annual turn-up, once again business cards can be included in package. Distribute newsletters with information about the latest offers and discounts.

Informational letters of a page length and e-mails can be sent too on a regular basis. All this can become lot easier by getting in touch with companies who can provide the mailing list of a particular locality and it comes for a very small price.

Again, yellow pages can be referred to get information about such companies. After getting information get in touch with company to get a copy of the latest mailing list.

Different companies charge different prices. The word of mouth is also a good method of advertising.

Try growing the links in your network and join organizations which deals with advertising like trade associations, chamber of commerce. Active participation in events of these organizations eventually helps reaching a greater number of people.

Conclusion

After the advent of online selling sites, shopping has been made so easy that it can be done within the comfort of the home.

Online selling gave rise to online advertising also known as Advertising, which is proving to be the best way to reach a larger audience within a short time using less money. There are many options available on the Internet to get started. Creating a website and then placing its link on different websites is one of the ways. Pages can be submitted to the search engines after applying search engine optimization techniques.

Websites offer various payment methods. Some take money for simply placing an ad or link on their website, some take money only if a visitor clicks on the link or website and some take money only if the visitors visits a link and have bought something or availed some service. There are options available for the type of ad being placed. There are pop-up ads, banner ads, wallpaper ads, polite ads, video ads, etc. Businesses with really low budget can send mails to targeted customers.

Radio stations offer a good price to advertise during the non-peak time. Get in touch with the local station and try to ask for a discount. The same applies to television; even they have a minimal amount for advertising slots during the non-prime hours, especially after midnight. Contact different television station to compare pricing.

The age-old tradition of advertising in yellow pages directories is always a success. All businesses from small to big register themselves in the yellow pages and have sworn to be benefited from it. People can look up for contact numbers, addresses and services offered directly from the pages.

Newspaper is the next best thing. First analyse the audience to be targeted by age group, sex, and location. Choose the local newspaper and section where the ad should be placed depending on the audiences to be targeted.

The classifieds department of the local newspapers have special offers, find out in detail about the pricing structure for the size of the advertisements, number of words, font size, etc.

Design the business cards with accuracy. Try to include all the vital information about the business like the name of the company, where it is located, services provided, working hours, and contact information like landline number, cell number and person to be contacted. Personalized business cards are good way of reaching the genuine customers. Other way to advertise is to give presentations on your products. Brochures can be inserted in business presentation package.

Other than things like history of the company and annual turn-up, once again business cards can be included in the package.

Distribute newsletters with information about the latest offers and discounts. Informational letters of a page length and e-mails can be sent too on a regular basis. All this can become lot easier by getting in touch with companies who can provide the mailing list of a particular locality and it comes for a very small price.

Again, the yellow pages can be referred to get information about such companies. After getting the information get in touch with company to get a copy of the latest mailing list. Different companies charge different prices.

The word of mouth is also a good method of advertising. Try growing the links in your network and join organizations which deals with advertising like trade associations and chamber of commerce. Active participation in events of these organizations eventually helps reaching a greater number of people.

CPSIA information can be obtained
at www.ICGtesting.com
Printed in the USA
BVHW042213130421
604819BV00009BA/984

9 781914 405112